MW01485386

How to Pray For Healing

A Practical Guide to

Answered Prayers

Rubens Cunha

ISBN 978-1-952170-00-3

CONTENTS

Introduction

God created us to enjoy perpetual wholeness in His presence. This is precisely the reason why no one wants to be sick. He gave us a divine aversion to sickness, even though the Fall of humankind through sin made our bodies vulnerable to decay and all sorts of afflictions.

The good news is that God addressed this issue in Christ's redemptive sacrifice on the cross by providing forgiveness of sins and healing to all that come to Him. Jesus repeatedly demonstrated His firm resolution to bring us divine health:

> *A large crowd followed Him, and He healed all who were ill. (Matthew 12:15)*

Jesus healed then and is still healing today.

The author of the book of Hebrews boldly declares that *"Jesus Christ is the same yesterday and today and* forever." *(Hebrews 13:8)*. He is the same everywhere, every day, and for everyone. Jesus has not changed, which means that He is still healing people like He did when He walked on the roads of Galilee.

This book is a manual on how to minister divine healing effectively. It draws upon the Bible and my hands-on, face-to-face experience of over twenty-five years praying for healing for hundreds of thousands around the world in our mass evangelistic campaigns. Through our ministry, real people such as yourself have experienced God's healing power, and Jesus has transformed many lives.

The ideas taught here will help you build a firm foundation of faith for miracles. After all, God is willing to do for you what He did and does for others. The biblical concepts shared in this book have helped me see my prayers answered; I am sure that if you apply them, they will help you too.

These principles are not meant to be used as some superstitious ritual or dogmatic formula. Divine healing flows through us because of our relationship with Christ. We are not "healers," your prayer or faith does not heal: Jesus is the healer.

Whether you are the person in need of healing or whether the person in need is a loved one or a stranger, the ministry of divine healing is simple: *God is the healer, and He heals because of His love, mercy, and compassion for us.* However, when we pray with faith, we become conduits of His grace: If you let him, He can use your life to heal the sick and set the captives free!

My invitation to you is that you read the coming chapters with an open mind and heart and that you understand and believe, unequivocally so, that God wants to use your life as a channel for His extraordinary miracles and to bring relief to those who suffer.

Every principle taught here will finish with an invitation to take action. Make sure you put into practice each step:

Take action

Pray and ask God to open your heart and mind so that you can understand the various biblical truths about divine healing discussed in this guidebook. Pray for love, compassion, and healing for the sick. Above all, as you pray, expect to receive a miracle!

Why we should expect healing

The Bible is full of examples of divine healing. The first record appeared in the book of Genesis when God healed several people in answer to Abraham's prayer:

> *Then Abraham prayed to God, and God healed Abimelek, his wife, and his female slaves so they could have children again. (Genesis 20:17)*

In the second book of the Bible, God delivered the Israelites from slavery and oppression in Egypt and took them to the Promised Land.

During their journey, God made a covenant with His people and declared:

> ... *I am the LORD who heals you.*
> *(Exodus 15:26)*

In this proclamation, we see both God's nature and will revealed. Healing is not just something that God does, but an intrinsic part of His character. This verse also tells us that He desires to heal you.

The people of Israel were not even praying for healing at that time, but God wanted them to understand that healing and wholeness are part of His essence. As a result of this revelation, there were none who were sick among the millions that left Egypt for the Promised Land.

> *He also brought them out with silver*
> *and gold, and there was none feeble*
> *among His tribes. (Psalm 105:37 NJKV)*

Unfortunately, the old covenant, made with the people of Israel in the desert as they traveled to

The Promised Land, was not sufficient because no one was able to live a perfectly holy life.

Thankfully, God put the old covenant aside and replaced it with a new and better one based on the perfect sacrifice of Jesus. Compared to the old one, the new covenant is superior since it is *"established on better promises"*:

> *But in fact, the ministry Jesus has received is as superior to theirs as the covenant of which He is mediator is superior to the old one, since the new covenant is established on better promises. (Hebrews 8:6)*

This is the covenant we enter into when we surrender our lives to Jesus.

If under the old and imperfect covenant, people would pray, expect, and receive healing, how much more should we expect healing now that we are living under a perfect covenant established by the blood of Jesus?

By His redemptive sacrifice on the cross, Jesus made provision for the healing of our bodies. Inspired by the Holy Spirit, Matthew quoted the prophet Isaiah and explained that Jesus' sacrifice was substitutionary, which means He took our place and suffered in our stead:

> *When evening came, many who were demon-possessed were brought to Him, and He drove out the spirits with a word and healed all the sick. This was to fulfill what was spoken through the prophet Isaiah: "He took up our infirmities and bore our diseases." (Matthew 8:16-17)*

When Jesus took our sins upon Himself on the cross, He also took our diseases. He paid the price for our complete and perfect redemption. Because of His sacrifice, divine healing belongs to us as a gift of God's grace to His people.

> *"He Himself bore our sins" in His body on the cross, so that we might die to sins*

and live for righteousness; "by His
wounds, you have been healed."
(1 Peter 2:24)

Healing the sick was a significant part of Jesus' proclamation of the arrival of God's Kingdom; about one-fifth of all the gospels focus on Jesus' healing ministry.

> *Jesus went throughout Galilee, teaching*
> *in their synagogues, proclaiming the*
> *good news of the kingdom, and healing*
> *every disease and sickness among the*
> *people. (Matthew 4:23)*

God gave Jesus the mission of proclaiming salvation and healing to everyone who wants it. Soon after starting His work, He shared this mission with His twelve disciples.

> *When Jesus had called the twelve*
> *together, He gave them power and*
> *authority to drive out all demons and to*
> *cure diseases, and He sent them out to*

> *proclaim the Kingdom of God and to*
> *heal the sick. (Luke 9:1-2)*

Jesus did not give or entrust this ministry of proclamation and healing exclusively to the twelve apostles; soon after, He appointed seventy-two others and sent them to the villages and towns ahead of Him with the same mission:

> *Heal the sick who are there and tell*
> *them, "The kingdom of God has come*
> *near to you." (Luke 10:9)*

The seventy-two disciples boldly proclaimed the Good News of the Kingdom and saw extraordinary miracles of healing and deliverance. It did not end there; after His resurrection, Jesus gave this mission to all His disciples in every place and every generation:

> *Go into all the world and preach the*
> *gospel to all creation. Whoever believes*
> *and is baptized will be saved, but*
> *whoever does not believe will be*

*condemned. **And these signs will accompany those who believe**: In my name, they will drive out demons; they will speak in new tongues; they will pick up snakes with their hands; and when they drink deadly poison, it will not hurt them at all; they will place their hands on sick people, and they will get well. (Mark 16:15-18 —emphasis added)*

This passage does not state that these signs will accompany pastors or missionaries or evangelists. It says these signs will accompany **"those who believe."** That means you!

Yes, you have the extraordinary privilege to participate in God's plan by sharing His Gospel and bringing healing in the name of Jesus!

Now that you understand why we should expect divine healing when we pray, I will share with you seven principles that have helped me, and that will help you pray for healing efficiently and in a way that allows you to see answered prayers.

Healing principle #1: Understand that you are not alone

In November 1994, I was speaking at a church in rural Brazil. At the time, I was hungry to see God's healing power in action, but my experiences had been disappointing. I was feeling confused and discouraged since many of the people I prayed for had not received healing.

What is the secret? I wondered to myself.

During that period, a particular Bible verse became alive to me and changed my entire life experience. That Bible verse was:

> *Then, the disciples went out and preached everywhere, and the Lord worked with them and confirmed His word by the signs that accompanied it. (Mark 16:20)*

By the grace of God, at that moment, I understood in my heart that divine healing happens because Jesus confirms His Gospel. It is not a result of my effort or personal holiness; it takes place exclusively because of Jesus' sacrifice on the cross.

When praying for healing, you need to understand and accept that we do not have an innate supernatural power to heal anyone. God, in the name of Jesus, and by the power of the Holy Spirit, is the healer. The astonishing thing about this is that God dwells in all those that surrendered their lives to Jesus!

God used the first disciples of Christ to perform extraordinary miracles. A great example of this occurred when Peter and John ministered healing to a paralytic man:

> *Then Peter said, "Silver or gold I do not have, but what I do have I give you. In the name of Jesus Christ of Nazareth, walk." Taking him by the right hand, he helped him up, and instantly the man's feet and ankles became strong. He jumped to his feet and began to walk. Then he went with them into the temple courts, walking and jumping, and praising God. (Acts 3:6-8)*

Faced with such a miracle, people reacted with great admiration, to which Peter said:

> *Fellow Israelites, why does this surprise you? Why do you stare at us as if by our own power or godliness we had made this man walk? (Acts 3:12)*

He then added:

> *By faith, in the name of Jesus, this man*
> *whom you see and know was made*
> *strong. It is Jesus' name and the faith*
> *that comes through Him that has*
> *completely healed him, as you can all*
> *see. (Acts 3:16)*

The first disciples experienced astounding miracles because they understood they were not alone; Jesus was living in them and working through them!

When we read Mark 16:20, it becomes clear that Jesus worked with His disciples to confirm the message of the Gospel through signs and wonders. He is the same yesterday, today, and forever. Because of this, He continues to work together with us to validate His Gospel the same way He did in the past.

The more conscious we are that **Jesus is the healer, and He lives in us**, the more we will witness God's supernatural healings. Miracles do not happen because of our efforts or good works; they happen because Jesus made the ultimate sacrifice for our redemption on the cross, triumphantly rose on the third day, and continues His mission through His disciples today.

Whenever we embark on praying for healing, we must become aware of Jesus' presence within us and trust that He will heal the sick through us now, just like He did through His first disciples. Trust the living presence of Jesus in you. Do your part sharing the Gospel and praying for healing, and He will work with you to confirm His message with beautiful miracles.

Take action

As you pray, practice the presence of Jesus by intentionally directing your affection to Him and becoming aware of His living presence in you.

Healing principle #2: Pray with expectant faith

In the book of James, we learn that if we are going to pray for the sick, we should pray with faith:

> And **the prayer offered in faith** will make the sick person well; the Lord will raise them up. If they have sinned, they will be forgiven.
> (James 5:15 - emphasis added)

It is not the lengthiest or the loudest prayer that accesses God's healing power; but rather the prayer that is offered in faith. Therefore, it is essential that you pray with resolute confidence in God's ability to restore health to those in need.

A formidable example is the healing of the paralytic man mentioned in the previous chapter. After Peter healed him in the name of Jesus, He said:

> *By faith, in the name of Jesus, this man whom you see and know was made strong. It is Jesus' name and the faith that comes through Him that has completely healed him, as you can all see. (Acts 3:16)*

God worked through Peter to restore the man's health because of his unwavering trust in Jesus. When you pray with expecting faith, God's wonders will flow through you too.

Faith is a confident expectation that God will meet our needs or the needs of others; it is the bridge that connects the provision of Heaven to the needs on earth. Biblical faith comes from understanding God's will as revealed in His Word:

> *So then faith comes by hearing, and*
> *hearing by the word of God.*
> *(Romans 10:17 NKJV)*

Therefore, it is imperative that you study the subject of divine healing in Scripture to grow your faith in this area.

It is also essential that you help the person in need of healing to fully trust God and His word. If we were to examine various healing narratives in the New Testament, we would be right to conclude that Jesus healed many people in response to their faith. This does not mean He is not sovereign; it means that in His sovereignty, He has decided to respond to how we trust Him in certain situations.

The healing of the woman with an issue of blood, as narrated in the Gospel of Mark, is a great example. This woman had suffered from severe bleeding for twelve years; she had spent everything she had on seeing doctors and seeking treatment, but her ailment only got worse with time.

One day, she heard about Jesus and believed that if she touched Him, a miraculous healing would happen. When Jesus was passing through her area, she pushed through the crowd, reached out, and when she touched Him in faith, healing power flowed from Jesus to the woman, who became instantly healed! Jesus acknowledged the power that had flowed out of Him and attested that the woman's faith was the catalyst for her miracle:

> *He said to her, "Daughter, your faith has healed you. Go in peace and be freed from your suffering." (Mark 5:34)*

Before she touched Jesus, she had the conviction that doing so would lead to her miraculous healing:

> *She thought, "If I just touch His clothes, I will be healed." (Mark 5:28)*

Multitudes have received extraordinary miracles in our evangelistic campaigns, and it is common to hear similar stories. Many have said in their hearts, "*I know that Jesus will heal me,*" and received a miracle of healing from God. Every single time I pray for healing in our campaigns, I say in my heart, "*Thank you, Jesus, for your healing power available to us and for healing people here today.*"

In the city of Maracanau, Brazil, a woman received a severe diagnosis of endometriosis and several other issues related to her digestive system. She had a surgery scheduled and had to take morphine every day so that she could be able to deal with the pain in her body.

When she heard about our pre-crusade conference, she went online intending to learn more about the ministry. She came across a video from our campaign in Pakistan, and faith stirred in her heart. She later confessed that at that moment, she said to her mother, *"I am going to the conference, and God will heal me."*

I remember that when she came for prayer at the end of the meeting, God healed her instantly and completely removed her pain! I will never forget the expression of relief on her face for the rest of my life. In a single moment, her suffering vanished. She wept and jumped for joy, and then prayed on her knees. Her family members hugged her, and they praised God together. It was a very moving moment.

Later on, she did a checkup and confirmed that all the medical conditions had disappeared. She activated her faith in the same way that the lady with the issue of blood from the Gospel story did; **in her heart, she had said that she was**

going to receive healing. She believed and received what Jesus conquered for her on the cross. What are you saying in your heart before you pray?

Build your faith and the faith of the sick person by studying and trusting God's word in the area of divine healing.

Take action:

Write down your favorite Bible verses on divine healing, meditate on them, and memorize them. Whenever you pray, do so with expecting faith and an unwavering assurance that God is with you, that He is listening to your prayer and will respond with a miracle.

Healing principle #3: Petition prayer

A petition is a request made to an authority. A petition prayer is a request to God, Jesus, or the Holy Spirit asking for help with our personal needs or the needs of someone else. Our requests for others are also called intercessory prayers. Jesus taught us:

> *Very truly, I tell you, my Father will give you whatever you ask in my name. (John 16:23)*

Prayer is an extraordinary privilege. By prayer, we can fellowship with our heavenly Father and enjoy a loving relationship with him. When we pray, we also affirm our submission to and dependence on God. In Scripture, many people received miracle healing through the petition prayers of others. A great example is the intercession of Jairus. He was a religious leader in the city of Capernaum, and his only daughter was very ill. He pleaded with Jesus to come and heal her: *"My little daughter is dying. Please come and put your hands on her so that she will be healed and live."* (Mark 5:23).

Jesus went with him, but when they arrived at Jairus' home, the little girl was already dead. Undaunted, Jesus entered into her room, took the dead girl by her hand, and said: *"Talitha koum!" (which means "Little girl, I say to you, get up!").* (Mark 5:41). She immediately stood up and began to walk around. Everyone was utterly astonished!

In another instance, the son of a royal official was sick. He came to Jesus and asked Him to heal his son, who was close to death. *"Go," Jesus replied, "your son will live."* (John 4:50). The man then returned home to find that his son was healed in the exact moment Jesus said: *"your son will live."*

Jesus is still answering petition prayers, and you can boldly ask Him to heal yourself or the people you are praying for.

> *"What do you want me to do for you?" Jesus asked him. The blind man said, "Rabbi, I want to see." "Go," said Jesus, "your faith has healed you." Immediately he received his sight and followed Jesus along the road. (Mark 10: 51-52)*

Jesus certainly knew that the man standing in front of Him was blind; why did He ask this question? Jesus gave him an opportunity to present his petition prayer before Him.

This is the confidence we have in approaching God: that if we ask anything according to His will, He hears us. (1 John 5:14)

When ministering to someone in need of healing, I usually ask, "*what do you need from Jesus?*". Then I pray in the name of Jesus and ask for a miracle. Jesus is still asking those in need: *"What do you want me to do for you?"*

Take action

When you pray for someone in need of healing, ask God for a miracle in the name of Jesus. As you pray, do that with a heart filled with expecting faith, and you will receive your answer.

Healing principle #4: The laying of hands

...they will place their hands on sick people, and they will get well. (Mark 16:18)

At sunset, the people brought to Jesus all who had various kinds of sickness, and laying His hands on each one, He healed them. (Luke 4:40)

The laying of hands is an act of obedience to the command of Christ and a point of contact for our faith. The Bible says that healing power came out of Jesus and healed the sick (Luke 6:19).

Jesus lives in each of us today; when we lay our hands on the sick, the power of the Holy Spirit and the virtue of divine healing flows from us and into the sick to heal them. When we lay our hands on others and pray, miracles happen!

When you pray for divine healing, lay your hands on the sick person, and trust that the power of the Holy Spirit that lives in you will flow to that person and destroy the power of sickness.

When laying hands, always remember to be respectful and loving towards the person receiving prayer. You do not need to put your hands directly on the sick part of the body, especially if you are praying for a stranger or a person of the opposite sex. If it makes you or the other person feel more comfortable, just lay your hands on the shoulders or the head of the person receiving prayer.

In one instance, I was teaching on healing at a conference. When I explained about the laying of hands, a man sitting in the audience decided he had learned enough. He immediately put his hand on a large growth he had had on his back for twenty years. That growth caused him a lot of discomfort and pain.

He prayed, *"Jesus, please release your healing power on my back now."* At that moment, he felt something like electricity coming out of his hands. The growth was gone! He was healed in the name of Jesus!

Take action

When you pray, lay your hands on the sick person with the understanding that **God gave you healing hands**. Believe that the power of the Holy Spirit will flow from you to heal the sick person just like it happened for Jesus.

Healing principle #5: Cast out the spirit of infirmity

When Jesus saw that a crowd was running to the scene, He rebuked the impure spirit. "You deaf and mute spirit," He said, "I command you, come out of him and never enter him again." The spirit shrieked, convulsed him violently, and came out. The boy looked so much like a corpse that many said, "he's dead." But Jesus took him by the

hand and lifted him to his feet, and he
stood up. (Mark 9:25-27)

On several occasions described in the Bible, Jesus healed the sick by expelling demonic spirits. It is interesting to realize that Jesus named the demonic spirits according to their destructive action. In the Bible passage above, Jesus used the expression 'deaf and mute spirit', which means that diseases can be caused by the direct action of demonic forces.

This spiritual truth may seem shocking to the Western mind, highly influenced by philosophies with a clear anti-supernatural bias. However, ignorance or denial of spiritual realities does not make them untrue.

The fact is that there are evil, spiritual entities that work to harm and destroy humanity. The Bible calls them demons; discernment of this spiritual reality will help you understand many of the afflictions that plague our society today.

Although these evil spiritual beings are real, you do not need to fear them. The Bible teaches that Jesus Christ of Nazareth has full authority over demonic powers, and He gave all believers His power and authority to defeat the Kingdom of Darkness. We fight in this spiritual warfare from a position of victory, and in the name of Jesus, we can cast out demons! If you would like to know more about this subject, please check my book *Deliverance Ministry*, a resource developed to help people understand and defeat demonic oppression in their lives and the lives of others.

There will be times when we can discern the works of a spirit of infirmity with ease; at other times, however, the source of the problem is not entirely clear. In any case, even when it is unclear, it is my practice to pray and cast out the spirit of infirmity, and I recommend you pray similarly. If you do, the miracles that will happen will no doubt amaze you.

Even though the demonic world is real, you must keep a balanced perspective. It is a mistake to ignore the spiritual warfare going around our lives, but it is also a mistake to think that all diseases are a result of demonic forces. We still live in a world plagued by bacteria, viruses, and other agents of disease. Either way, God heals!

I pray for deliverance in all our campaigns. Typically, during these events, hundreds of oppressed people receive freedom every night. One of the most dramatic deliverances I witnessed took place at a campaign organized in the Brazilian state of Sergipe and involved a young woman diagnosed with epilepsy, schizophrenia, and several other mental issues.

The woman was from a poor family; and because of the financial and cultural limitations to care for her mentally ill daughter, the mother had to chain her to the bed every night. Can you imagine the pain of having to chain your own child to a bed every night? Her story was truly heartbreaking. She came to the first night of the campaign, and during the prayers for healing and deliverance, several demonic spirits manifested and were cast out. After the demons left her, she had a perfectly sound mind, and all symptoms instantly disappeared!

The next day, her mother felt so excited that she took her to a doctor in the state capital. They did an MRI test, and the mother brought the results to the campaign. The brain lesions previously identified as a cause for her seizures and mental issues had disappeared. The girl smiled and told the crowd how great she felt. Faith, in the mighty name of Jesus, healed her.

Take action:

When you pray, cast out the spirit of infirmity. For example, if you are praying for a deaf person, you can say *"deaf spirit, I command you to leave now. In Jesus' name, come out now!"*

Never forget that in spiritual warfare, we always fight from a position of victory in Christ.

Healing principle #6: Prayer of command

> *"But I want you to know that the Son of Man has authority on earth to forgive sins." So He said to the paralyzed man, "I tell you, get up, take your mat and go home." Immediately he stood up in front of them, took what he had been lying on and went home praising God. (Luke 5: 24-25)*

A worthwhile thing to note is that most of the healing miracles Jesus and the apostles performed were not a result of a petition prayer but the result of a prayer of command spoken with spiritual authority, as the verse above illustrates.

The prayer of command is by far the most used type of prayer to minister healing in the New Testament; unfortunately, it is the least used today, and we need to change that. Here are several other examples of prayer of command in action:

1. Jesus healed the man with the shriveled hand by commanding, *"stretch out your hand."* (Matthew 12:13)

2. Peter ministered healing to the paralytic man at the temple gate by saying, *"In the name of Jesus Christ of Nazareth, walk."* (Acts 3: 6-7)

3. Peter ministered healing to Aeneas, the paralytic of Lydda, by saying,

"Jesus Christ heals you. Get up and roll up your mat." (Acts 9:34)

4. Paul ministered healing to a man who was lame from birth by speaking, *"Stand up on your feet!"* (Acts 14:10)

In the name of Jesus, we have the authority to speak to circumstances and diseases and call miracles into existence!

As part of our evangelistic work, we go door-to-door in low-income areas of the world to donate food and share the Gospel. In one of these outreaches, a little girl of around five years old grabbed my hand and asked, *"can you please pray for my grandmother?"* The child's faith was moving. I answered, *"of course,"* and we walked to her home.

In the living room, a lady who looked to be around sixty years old sat on an old couch. She seemed to be very sick. Her face was downcast, and her eyes showed she was in great pain. I asked her what she needed from Jesus, and she explained that she had many issues. Her body hurt in many places and she was not able to walk on her own.

After praying for her, she experienced immediate relief. She managed to stand up and walk by herself. She felt surprised by the miracle; encouraged by the improvement she felt, she asked, *"my right eye is blind, can you pray for it?"*. *"Sure!"* I said and laid hands on her eyes.

I remember clearly that I first thanked God for His love and healing power and then spoke: *"Eye open, in the name of Jesus!"* At that moment, she saw a bright light, and when she opened her eye, she could see clearly again! Her family felt shocked and could not deny the reality of God's presence in their home. I shared the Gospel with them, and the entire family decided to follow Christ. What a wonderful God we serve!

Take action

Whenever you pray for healing, speak to the problem in faith and give a word of command just as Jesus and His first disciples did.

Speak to the body part that is sick and exercise authority in the name of Jesus, commanding restoration into that part. For example, you can say, *"Deaf ear, in the name of Jesus, open and start hearing now."*

Healing principle #7: Put faith in action

In Lystra there sat a man who was lame. He had been that way from birth and had never walked. He listened to Paul as he was speaking. Paul looked directly at him, saw that he had faith to be healed, and called out, "Stand up on your feet!" At that, the man jumped up and began to walk. (Acts 14:8-10)

Many of those healed in the New Testament and even today received their miracle when they put their faith in action. That is when, by faith, they began to do what they could not do before, they received healing.

When Paul commanded the crippled man in Lystra to stand up, the man did not wait for someone to pick him up, nor did he expect to feel 'something different.' He simply jumped up and began to walk. He put His faith in action and received a great miracle!

In our evangelistic campaigns, I always give people a chance to put their faith in action by saying this at the end of the prayer, *"In the name of Jesus, do now what you could not do before."* During this moment of prayer, thousands of people have received great miracles from God.

Whenever you pray for healing, encourage those receiving prayer to put their faith in action by doing what they could not do before. Do it with love and never force a situation. Respect the level of faith displayed by each person.

While on a campaign in Ethiopia, a woman put her faith in action and received an extraordinary miracle. She was unable to stand or walk and used to drag herself around her small village. She heard about the salvation and healing campaign happening in her city and dragged her diseased legs through several miles of dusty roads to arrive at the large open field where we held our campaign. I did not know that she was there, but Jesus did.

He saw her and felt compassionate towards her, the same compassion He has for all sick people. I finished praying for healing and addressed the crowd saying, *"in the name of Jesus, put your faith in action and do now what you could not do before."* That woman felt the power of God moving through her body and jumped to her feet; she was astonished when she realized that she could walk! She came running to the platform so excited that it was difficult to take her testimony, she jumped, ran back and forth, and even danced for joy. The crowd of over thirty thousand people shouted for joy and praised God with great enthusiasm. Jesus is truly alive!

Take action

When you finish a prayer for healing, tell the person receiving prayer to do that which he or she could not do before. For example, if the issue was a pain in the arm, say, "*now raise your arm in the name of Jesus.*" If the pain was in the leg, say, "*move your leg in the name of Jesus,*" and so on.

Next, I will answer some common questions that most people have about sickness and healing.

7 important questions about divine healing

We just learned seven powerful principles that you can use to pray for divine healing. In this chapter, I will discuss with you seven of the most common questions I hear on this subject.

#1: Does God make people sick?

No, God does not make people sick. The Bible has no instance of Jesus causing someone to fall ill.

God revealed Himself as the healer of all diseases (Exodus 15:26). It would be a contradiction if He were the healer and, at the same time, the author of diseases. The Bible says:

> *Every good and perfect gift is from*
> *above, coming down from the Father of*
> *the heavenly lights, who does not*
> *change like shifting shadows.*
> *(James 1:17)*

Diseases are definitely not good or perfect gifts.

Furthermore, if diseases were God's will, it would be a grave sin of rebellion to visit a doctor or to take medication. Clinics and hospitals would be places of disobedience and rebellion, which would not make any sense at all! God does not make you sick; He heals you.

> *God anointed Jesus of Nazareth with*
> *the Holy Spirit and power, and how He*
> *went around doing good and healing*

*all who were under the power of the
devil because God was with him.
(Acts 10:38)*

#2: Can someone lose his healing?

Yes, under certain conditions, it is possible.

On one occasion, Jesus healed a paralyzed man
and later told him:

> *See, you are well again. Stop sinning,
> or something worse may happen to
> you. (John 5:14)*

In other words, unconfessed sins open the door
for sickness to return. Healing is part of God's
plan of salvation, and He is interested in our
complete transformation. We need to invite
people to a life of surrender and obedience to
Christ.

Redemption gives us many blessings in this life,
but God's highest purpose is the salvation of the
soul. When we surrender our lives to Christ, He

forgives our sins, and we receive the gift of eternal life. Eternity with God is more important than any other blessing in this world.

By the way, never forget that it is not our place to judge if someone is in sin or not. Our responsibility is to love and share the Gospel.

Unbelief also can cause a person to lose his or her healing.

Peter experienced an amazing miracle when Jesus called him to walk on water. However, Peter took his eyes off Jesus, became afraid of the wind, and began to sink (Matthew 14:29). In other words, he doubted and lost his miracle. Unbelief and doubt can cause a person to lose his or her healing.

The good news is that when Peter was sinking, he cried out to Jesus, and He stretched out His hand to help him. We have a loving Father who is willing to help us in our struggles. If you or someone else is struggling with faith for healing, continue to study the Word of God and to build your faith.

A demonic attack can cause people to lose their miracle if they believe the lies of the enemy and do not stand on their healing by faith. At times, miraculous healing is a process of spiritual warfare that requires perseverance in prayer and confidence in God's Word.

The Bible says the devil is a thief who tries to steal God's blessings in our lives (John 10:10). The enemy may try to attack with fear or fake symptoms. In this case, engage in spiritual warfare by casting out the spirit of infirmity and its lies. Take a stand against the powers of darkness in the name of Jesus.

Poor stewardship of our bodies also can cause the return of a sickness.

The Bible tells us that our bodies are temples of the Holy Spirit (1 Corinthians 6:19), and we need to be guardians of our bodies. A poor choice in eating habits or lifestyle will make the body vulnerable to diseases. It is wise and God-honoring to make healthier lifestyle choices.

#3: Can I pray for healing and still go to a doctor?

Yes, divine healing and medical science are not in conflict. Divine healing is the process God uses to remove sickness from your body through His supernatural power. Medicine-based healing is the process God uses to remove sickness from your body through doctors, medication, and healthy lifestyle choices.

Either way, all healing comes from God, and it is therefore not wrong for a Christian to see a physician or to take medication. They are not in conflict. Believe and pray for your healing and see a doctor if you have to.

The Bible does not condemn medical science. Scripture positively refers to ancient medical remedies in several passages, such as in the parable of the good Samaritan when Jesus says the compassionate traveler used bandages, wine and olive oil to take care of the wounded man (Luke 10:34). The apostle Paul calls Luke "*the beloved physician*" (Colossians 4:14).

#4: Are some healings gradual?

Yes, the Bible shows that Jesus healed people all the time, but not all the healings happened instantaneously. The Gospels have several narratives of gradual healing. For example, Jesus prayed for a blind man, he started to see, but his vision was still blurry. He prayed a second time, and the man became fully healed (Mark 8:22-25).

On another occasion, Jesus healed ten men infected with leprosy by telling them to show themselves to the priests. "*And as they went, they were cleansed.*" (Luke 17:14). The healing happened "*as they went.*" John tells the story of the healing of the son of a royal official. Jesus told him, "*Your son will live.*" Later, servants said that his son *"got better"* when Jesus had determined His healing (John 4:52). *"Got better"* means his healing was gradual; it did not happen instantly.

Sometimes we pray but do not experience the results instantly; that does not mean that the person was not healed. It could mean that healing is taking place gradually.

In almost every campaign we hold, we hear testimonies of persons that felt better immediately, and after a short period, were completely healed. It is also common that some people do not feel any different, but they go home, and discover that they are healed on the next day.

In a recent campaign in Brazil, a woman had a tumor the size of a soccer ball under her right arm. The tumor was so large that she could not rest her arm against her body. There was no visual improvement during the prayer, and she went home feeling disappointed. The next morning, when she woke up, she moved her arm and realized the tumor had disappeared!

Even if there is no apparent improvement, encourage the person you prayed for to keep their faith alive in Jesus and explain that sometimes healing is a process.

#5: Is it OK to pray more than once?

Yes, it is. Even Jesus prayed twice for a man who needed healing:

> *They came to Bethsaida, and some people brought a blind man and begged Jesus to touch him. He took the blind man by the hand and led him outside the village. When He had spit on the man's eyes and put His hands on him, Jesus asked, "Do you see anything?" He looked up and said, "I see people; they look like trees walking around." Once more, Jesus put His hands on the man's eyes. Then his eyes opened, and his*

*sight restored; He saw everything
clearly. (Mark 8:22-25)*

In my experience, there have been several occasions that persons received healing after a second or third prayer. In some circumstances, I prayed for several days as the person's health improved gradually.

#6: Who does God want to heal?

God wants to heal everyone.

> *When evening came, many who were demon-possessed were brought to Him, and He drove out the spirits with a word and **healed all the sick**.
> (Matthew 8:16- emphasis added)*

> *A large crowd followed Him, and He **healed all who were ill**.
> (Matthew 12:15 - emphasis added)*

Jesus healed everyone that came to Him. The Bible says that God shows no favoritism (Acts

10:34). If He wanted to heal one person without healing the other, it would mean that He has favorites. Healing is not a lottery for a few privileged; it is a blessing from a loving Father to all His children.

Jesus healed everyone that came to him. In the entire Bible, the only person that questioned if it was God's will for him to receive healing was a man with leprosy, a terrifying and contagious disease that caused severe disfigurement and nerve damage. His story is in the book of Mark:

> *Now a leper came to Him, imploring Him, kneeling down to Him and saying to Him, "If you are willing, you can make me clean." Then Jesus, moved with compassion, stretched out His hand and touched him, and said to him, "I am willing; be cleansed." As soon as He had spoken, immediately, the leprosy left him, and he was cleansed. (Mark 1:40-42 NKJV)*

Jesus was willing then just as He is willing now. The compassion Jesus had for the leper is the same He has for all that are sick. He wants to heal all!

#7: **Who can pray for the sick?**

Every believer in Jesus Christ has the authority to pray for healing. Some denominations mistakenly believe that only church officials and ministers are allowed to pray for healing. This misunderstanding comes from a passage in the book of James:

> *Is anyone among you sick? Let them call the elders of the church to pray over them and anoint them with oil in the name of the Lord. (James 5:14)*

In this verse, the Bible is not saying that only the church elders can pray for healing. Instead, it means that, in the context of a local church, its leaders should always be available to pray for those in need.

The mission to pray for healing is entrusted to every believer. You don't have to be an ordained minister or go to Bible School for several years to be used by God to pray for miracles and help people. In the Gospels, as well as in the book of Acts, we read many reports of ordinary Christians healing people in the name of Jesus. For example, Ananias prayed for Paul, and he was healed of his blindness (Acts 9:17-19).

Every single disciple of Jesus has the authority to release divine healing. Who can pray for the sick? **You can**. **You have the permission and the commission from Jesus.**

> *As the Father has sent me, I am sending you. (John 20:21)*

Heal the sick in Jesus' name

*And these signs will accompany those
who believe: In my name, they will
drive out demons; they will speak in
new tongues; they will pick up snakes
with their hands; and when they drink
deadly poison, it will not hurt them at
all; they will place their hands on sick
people, and they will get well.*
(Mark 16: 17-18)

Jesus gave the ministry of healing and deliverance to all His disciples. This ministry does not depend on our merits or efforts; it happens because of Jesus' perfect sacrifice at the cross. As a disciple of Christ, you are a messenger of God sent to proclaim salvation and demonstrate His power in our generation.

Start praying for the sick, and you will embark on a life-changing journey that will help many have an encounter with God in our generation.

Here is a summary of the principles we learned and the most frequent questions I hear about divine healing:

A recap of the key principles to use when ministering healing

1. Pray with the awareness that Jesus is in you and works through you.

2. Pray with expectant faith and build faith in the person in need of healing by sharing truth found in Scripture.

3. Make a petition prayer; ask God, Jesus, or the Holy Spirit to heal the sick person.

4. Lay hands on the sick. Remember that the Holy Spirit lives in you, and when you lay your hands on the sick, His healing power flows from you and into the sick.

5. Cast out the spirit of infirmity. Jesus gave you authority over demonic powers.

6. Use the prayer of command. By faith, command the healing to take place in the name of Jesus.

7. Put faith in action. After you pray, tell the person to do what he or she could not do before.

Key takeaways from frequently asked questions about healing

1. God does not make people sick; He heals people.

2. A person can lose his or her healing due to sin, unbelief, a spiritual warfare attack, or poor stewardship of the body.

3. Medical science is not in opposition or conflict with divine healing; they work together well.

4. Some people receive healing instantly; others do so gradually.

5. It is okay to pray more than once for someone who needs healing.

6. God wants to heal everyone.

7. Jesus authorized every believer to heal the sick.

It is your turn now. Put your faith in action; go and heal the sick in Jesus' name!

Thank you for reading *How to Pray for Healing*. If you enjoyed this book, please go to Amazon.com and leave a review. This will encourage others to benefit from the information and encouragement found within these pages.

About the author

Rubens Cunha is a Brazilian born missionary evangelist, author and international speaker who has led hundreds of thousands to Christ around the world through massive evangelistic campaigns.

His global evangelistic ministry is marked by an impressive healing anointing after the model of Jesus: proclamation and demonstration of the salvation message with signs and wonders. Many have received miracle healing at these events, but even more importantly: multitudes have experienced salvation and peace through Jesus Christ. In his campaigns, Rubens boldly proclaims that Jesus Christ is the same every day, everywhere and for everyone (Hebrews 13:8).

Rubens holds a Bachelor of Theology and a postgraduate degree in New Testament Theology.

Above: In Codo, Brazil, Jesus confirmed His Gospel with many extraordinary healing miracles.

Below: Gospel Festival in Codo, Brazil. Thousands gathered to hear the Gospel.

Above: A young man healed of blindness demonstrates his miracle.

Below: Rubens Cunha sharing the Gospel in the Amazon region.

Made in the USA
Monee, IL
24 September 2020